THE SPIRIT EMPOWERING LIFE

APOSTLE SAMMY N. ADDY

THE SPIRIT EMPOWERING LIFE

Copyright © 2014 by Apostle Sammy N. Addy

The Spirit Empowering Life
By Apostle Sammy N. Addy

Printed in the United States of America

ISBN: 10: 1940260043
ISBN: 13: 978-1-940260-04-4

All rights reserved solely by the author. The author guarantees all contents are original and do not infringe upon the legal rights of any other person or work. No part of this publication may be reproduced or transmitted in any form or by any means without written permission of the publisher. The views expressed in this book are not necessarily those of the publisher.

Unless otherwise indicated, Bible quotations are taken from the King James Bible and Amplified Bible Copyright © 2014

Cover Design By: Faith Walley

Published By:
Cibunet Publishing
P. O. Box 444
Woodlawn, NY 10470
Email: admin@cibunet.com
Website: www.cibunet.com

THE SPIRIT EMPOWERING LIFE

TABLE OF CONTENTS

ACKNOWLEGEMENT.................................7

DEDICATION...9

FOREWORD..10

CHAPTER ONE
The Advantage of God's Children.....................13

CHAPTER TWO
Developing Our Potential...............................21

CHAPTER THREE
The Word as a Mirror....................................31

CHAPTER FOUR
The Tragedy of the Church.............................43

CHAPTER FIVE
Role of the Word of God................................53

CHAPTER SIX
Understanding Worship..................................61

CHAPTER SEVEN
Importance of the Word of God..........................65

CHAPTER EIGHT
Memorize and Meditate on the Word of God.....71

CHAPTER NINE
Speak the Word of God.....................................79

CHAPTER TEN
Apply the Word of God......................................85

ACKNOWLEDGEMENTS

I am thankful to Bishop N. A. Tackie-Yarboi, the presiding Bishop of Victory Bible Church International, for giving me the foundation in scripture. You are a great spiritual father.

To Bishop Eric A. McDaniel of the Lord's Church Family Worship Center, Bishop Pasival Fafalie Selly of Word Aflame Family Chapel, Bishop Michael A. Frith of Family of Christ Church and Reverend Dr. Joseph Baisie of Transcontinental Assemblies of God Church, thank you for trusting me enough to allow me to be part of your ministries.

I thank Reverends Eugene and Thomasina Wright for their love for me and what I do; Reverend Dr. Patricia Rekenbekka without whom I could have been a loner and lost in the big city of New York— God bless you for watching my back.

Thanks to Apostle William and Pastor Belinda Shalders for their unending friendship. To Ms Theresa Black of Esperanza Center for giving me the opportunity to experience the field of developmental disability in New York City; the experience has been enormous, thanks. To my covenant brother,

Alexander K. Archine of Oak Financial Services Ltd, for sticking with me when we both did not know what the future held for us.

I am grateful to all the staff, members and partners of Wisdom Chapel International in the Bronx and Wisdom International Network Ministries, especially Elder Esther Tackie and Pastor Jermyn Addy for your unceasing support; Also to Jerry Zimmerman for giving me space to operate my ministry without stress.

I cannot show enough appreciation and gratitude to Patience Kwao-Sarbah, David Kwao-Sarbah and Jason Addy for making this book become a reality and following through to the end.

To all my sons and daughters in ministry and the numerous people who believe in me, I appreciate your unconditional love and support.

May Jehovah increase you more and more.

DEDICATION

To my dear friend and partner in ministry, my wife and mother of my children—both spiritual and natural—Adeline Addy and my four sons Jermyn, Julian, Jason and Jeffron whose endless support and belief in me has brought about a powerful ministry. Thanks for what you do to keep the fire burning.

To my mom and dad, Emmanuel Obo Addy and Patience Tsuishitoo Addy, for the training and foundation you gave me as a child to sharpen my character and destiny by preparing me for life. May your souls rest in perfect peace, you are the best parents one could have.

To all ministers of the gospel who are contemplating throwing in the towel. It is too late to quit now. His gifts and callings are irrevocable so maximize the grace over your life and God will open new doors of opportunities for you. Keep fighting forward.

FOREWORD

The times in which we find ourselves as a generation, calls for renewed emphasis on the power of the 'logos' word working alongside 'rhema' revelations from the Holy Spirit to produce the powerful life that is characteristic of a spirit-filled believer. Satan's agenda to neutralize the Christian believer to live a 'commonsense' lifestyle, has taken root in Pentecostal and Charismatic circles such that, it is difficult to tell the difference between the saved and the unsaved. Unfortunately, the Church is working so hard to become 'mainstream', which is today's popular term for spiritual compromise.

We are so inclined on creating an atmosphere that attracts everyone to the Church and left behind the core values of our salvation. The Apostle Paul mentioned in Romans 1:16&17 that "...the gospel is the power of God unto salvation for everyone that believeth... for therein is the righteousness of God revealed from faith to faith." The gospel is the key to unveiling the power of God's righteousness that makes the believer a totally different person with the supernatural ability to impact the world in a unique way. We are called to "build the old wastes, raise up the former desolations and repair the waste cities."

THE SPIRIT EMPOWERING LIFE

This renaissance is what Apostle Sammy Addy has been burdened to restore to today's believer in this book and I trust that as you read it, you will be renewed in your passion to apply divine truths once again to all areas of your life.

Dr. Kenneth Walley
Senior Pastor of Power Chapel, President of KWI and Cibunet Corporation

THE SPIRIT EMPOWERING LIFE

CHAPTER ONE

THE SPIRIT EMPOWERING LIFE

The Advantage of God's Children

"For the law of the spirit of life in Christ Jesus hath made me free from the law of sin and death. For what the law could not do, in that it was weak through the flesh, God sending his own son in the

likeness of sinful flesh, and for sin, condemned sin in the flesh: that the righteousness of the law might be fulfilled in us, who walk not after the flesh, but after the spirit"

Romans 8:2-4

Several years ago, before I became born again, little did I know that one could live a normal life without depending on alcohol or illicit drugs. For me, a typical Friday morning was to plan how the weekend was going to be like. Together with my friends, I would go as far as travelling from one city to the next looking for opportunity to party. I depended on any substance that could make me feel high, until I realized that those substances were making me hallucinate and I had become quite paranoid in my attitude.

Before I got to this point, I thought that intoxication was the climax of enjoying life. The idea of following Christ and his teaching was farfetched. In my mind, one would have to be perfect and get rid of every bad habit to be able to develop and build a relationship with Christ.

One day, on my way to visit a friend, I met another friend who spoke to me about Christ and the concept of being born again. Because I thought it was impossible to have a relationship with a divine God in our humanity, I hesitated and asked him how it could be possible for a sinful man to develop a relationship with a deity. He took his time and explained how Christ came to this earth with the sole purpose of reconciling humanity back to God.

In our humanness, we sometimes miss out on the benefits that God has for us because we always follow the proclivity of our flesh. That is, the flesh drives us to act carnally rather than spiritually. In order to overcome the flesh and stay spiritual, it is important to seek spiritual renewal.

We cannot reach our full potential by living a life in the flesh or living by chance. Some people wish for certain results all their lives, and are not able to reach those goals because they do not take active and positive steps to reach those goals. Life expectations cannot be attained by merely wishing, nor do we prosper by aspiring. These always call for careful planning and determination.

To be successful, one has to plan. There is a popular saying that if you fail to plan, you are planning to fail. People plan and prepare to win championships. They sacrifice their time, lay other things which are not of importance aside, train themselves and do all they can to ensure that they position themselves for the desired results. For such people, when the opportunity comes, they are ready for it.

God wants us to understand that to be able to have the best in life, we do not have to walk by our natural carnal abilities only. We rather have to first seek spiritual development and then when we have mastered the spiritual life, the natural aspects will fall into place. Since the supernatural dimension of life rules over the natural, if you develop your spirit being you have an advantage in the natural. This is because the spirit cannot be limited, but the natural aspect of our being is limited only to this physical realm. The spiritually developed person can benefit from both the spiritual and physical realms.

God has given us that advantage to experience life both spiritually and naturally as His children. When Christ came, what He came to teach us was to live in both realms.

Christ ate when He was hungry and needed food, but there were times He told His followers, *"Man shall not live by bread alone" Matthew 4:4.* He was telling them that food is good. It is good to eat burgers and all the exotic foods that we enjoy as humans, but the spirit also needs to be fed and what the spirit feeds on is the word of God.

As much as our physical body needs nourishment to grow, Jesus said that man shall not live by food alone, but by every word that proceeds from the mouth of God. Jesus is drawing our attention to the reality of focusing also on the spirit form. Without our spirit, our physical being cannot survive the onslaughts of the Devil. Christ is telling us to live a balanced life because we are not just physical human beings but rather we are spiritual beings with the physical aspect of our being aspiring for the best earthly experiences.

When we take advantage of the death, burial and resurrection of Christ Jesus, every believer uniquely benefits from an infusion of divinity into our humanity. This was our original state of existence before the sin of Adam betrayed the whole human race. Christ came purposely to show us how to live both the spiritual and physical life.

If Christ did not come to redeem us from our own self destructive ways, we cannot attain that dimension of a flourishing life as humans with a divine nature. He took on a human form to exemplify how to live the spirit life. This is the advantage we have over other religious people. Whilst most religions teach their following of a goal of trying to reach to God, Jesus Christ has already made a way for us to relate to God as spirit beings.

THE SPIRIT EMPOWERING LIFE

We simply have to accept the sacrifice of His life on the cross on our behalf. By accepting all that He came to do for us, we have the advantage to live the life of God just like Adam did before the fall.

"For as much as the children are partakers of flesh and blood, he took part of the same; that through death he might destroy him that had power of death, that is the devil; and deliver them who through fear of death were all their life time subject to bondage. For verily he took not on him the nature of angels; but he took on him the seed of Abraham"
Hebrews 2:14-16

Christ could not have taken on the nature of angels because angels do not have jurisdiction over the earth realm. The only nature that could qualify him to be introduced to our world was to live through flesh and blood just as any human, so that he could redeem us from the indictment of sin.

"According as his divine power hath given unto us all things that pertain unto life and godliness, through the knowledge of him that hath called us to glory and virtue: whereby are given unto us exceeding great and precious promises: that by these ye might be partakers of the divine nature, having escaped the corruption that is in the world through lust"
2 Peter1:3&4

THE SPIRIT EMPOWERING LIFE

To be a partaker of his divine nature is to be part of his spirit life. God is a spirit and we can only relate to him in the spirit so he gave His son to introduce us to the spirit life. Through his death, burial and resurrection, the spirit life was introduced to humanity, and anyone who identifies with Jesus Christ may no longer live a mere natural life, but experience the privilege of a supernatural life in Christ.

Chapter Two

THE SPIRIT EMPOWERING LIFE

Developing Our Potential

"For the earnest expectation of the creature waiteth for the manifestation of the sons of God"
                                                              Romans 8:19

THE SPIRIT EMPOWERING LIFE

The whole creation is waiting for God's children to mature into their full potential as spirit beings to take dominion over creation. Not long after I became saved, I visited a crusade organized by one of the Christian organizations in my city and heard a powerful teaching from the late renown preacher, Dr. T. L. Osborne, whom I consider one of God's choice servants. There were a lot of miracles, signs and wonders. The lame walked, the mute spoke for the first time and numerous people were healed from their infirmities. After the crusade, I marvelled at how he was able to articulate the Word of God with such great power and clarity that after his message, numerous people responded to accept Christ as their Savior and Lord.

I was challenged by the extraordinary life of Dr. T. L. Osborne and how he manifested the supernatural power of God. Without a shadow of doubt I realized that it was the power of God at work in him. He did not claim to have acquired this ability by a secret ritual, but rather admitted to simply accepting Christ as his Savior and developing a life of faith in God's word.

I became deeply inspired and began a diligent quest of reading and studying the word of God with occasional fasting. The more I developed myself through studying God's word, I realised that there was a zeal that erupted from within that pushed me to do more for the kingdom of God and for the course of Christ more than I had ever done. To say the least, I realized that all my efforts led me to do what I thought I could not do before. My spirit matured to a point of taking on challenges that I would not have taken, if I had not developed my spiritual life.

In order to rise to the fullness of our potential, we need to focus on our spiritual life and not just the natural. We must not live our lives by just eating food and drinking wine that only caters to our humanity. It is important to sometimes take time out, abstain from physical comforts and focus on the Word that proceeds out of the mouth of God. Through fasting, prayer and allowing the word of God to renew our thinking to align us to God's will, we will plunge ourselves into spiritual renewal which is important for the development of our spirit being.

Beyond our human understanding of the natural, there is also the vast realm of the spiritual with endless possibilities and great aspects that we need to gain a grasp of, in order to experience its potential influences on our existence. The spiritual realm holds the key to ailments that plague us for which we have no medical solution, psychological problems that inhibit our ability to achieve greatness, as well as

THE SPIRIT EMPOWERING LIFE

scientific debacles that remain a mystery to researchers.

Every now and then, we are able to make discoveries and inventions that push our advancement in technology to overcome crude ways of achieving goals. It is as though we are attempting to catch up with knowledge that has always been available, yet we have to suffer so much until the researching human mind is able to comprehend what has always been. There is no need to wait a thousand years to discover what is already in existence in the spiritual realm. We simply have to accept the divine nature of God by accepting the work of Christ on the cross of Calvary. It is our key to divinity and the experience of the supernatural ability to foster change quicker than all human ability can achieve within the space of time.

The divine potentials residing in us are the elements of our existence that always require renewal. Renewal starts from within and eventually shows outwards. It is inside out rather than outside in. Naturally we focus more on the outside, because Adam's disobedience made us more carnal than spiritual.

Most of our efforts in life are geared toward survival in the face of challenges instead of engaging our supernatural abilities. We were created in the image and likeness of God to experience dominion in life. We need to use the potentials we have received from our union with Christ. This is because when we accept Christ into our lives, the God nature which makes us spiritual is renewed in us. *"he that is joined to the Lord is one spirit...."*

Let us talk a little about professional development as well as personal development. Professional development relates to how you handle yourself on the job, how you deal with your clients and how you sell yourself. While professional development positions us to earn an income with which we may procure the good things of life, it is also obvious that a good income is not necessarily the key to a happy existence. There are so many people out there who have a lot of money in their bank accounts, yet are constantly battling with depression, strange medical conditions, marital frustrations, psychological inhibitions, family dysfunctions just to name a few. No amount of money gained from professional development can change some of the prevalent challenges we face as individuals and society as a whole.

Personal development on the other hand is a factor that positions us for wholeness as human beings. If you do not develop yourself spiritually, you could be professionally successful but still be lacking. For

THE SPIRIT EMPOWERING LIFE

instance you can have all the material things you want but may not have good relationships with people so it becomes impossible to enjoy life to its fullness. Though you may work hard and make millions of dollars, without personal development, it is difficult and almost impossible to keep a family and you may end up as a victim of a broken home. Personal life development is how you groom your spirit life to have a relationship with God through salvation in Christ.

God wants us to live a balanced life. He wants us to reach our full potential to demonstrate how a great God can take an ordinary human life and reveal His awesome glory as He did with Christ Jesus whilst on earth. The aim of this book is to help you rise above the limitations that this natural life places on all and develop yourselves to become fully matured sons and daughters of God.

Most often the natural life can make us feel disadvantaged because of the difficulties and hardships we go through. Christ did not promise us a stress free life. He said in the world we will have tribulations, but we should be of good cheer because he has overcome for us.

"These things I have spoken unto you, that in me ye might have peace. In the world ye shall have

tribulation: but be of good cheer; I have overcome the world"

John 16:33

Christ assures us that God has given us all things that pertain to life and Godliness so that our lives can become enhanced with better abilities in order to manifest his glory as his children. Spiritual enlightenment positions us to take advantage of these privileges.

Victory in life hinges strongly on perspective. A drinking glass can either be half empty or half full based on how you look at it. Those who see it as half-empty have that measure of partial advantages in the face of life's situations, while those with a half-full view can tackle challenges with the fullness of human and divine resources.

If your perspective on life is always in the negative, no matter what positive comes your way, you may still interpret it as negative. In order to enjoy the fullness of life, it is important that you develop a positive perspective by focusing on the promises of God in His word rather than the challenges that so often besets us.

There are many people who are saddled constantly with mind-sets of negative perspectives even in church. When you attempt to motivate them, all they say is, "oh but..." When you talk about the benefits of being God's children such people are quick to raise pessimistic "ifs" and "buts". Have you come across people like that? It is so tough to get such people to trust God for the great things in life. For them, the full meaning of Christ's coming is yet to have the intended impact.

Being open to the transforming power of God's word is key to overcoming negative mind-sets. The scripture says that the word of God is quick and powerful and sharper than any two edged sword. It pierces to establish clarity between soul and spirit as well as bone, joint and marrow.

"For the word of God is quick, and powerful, and sharper than any two-edged sword, piercing even to the dividing asunder of soul and spirit, and of the joints and marrow, and is a discerner of the thoughts and intents of the heart"
Hebrews 4:12

If you are open to God's word as the final authority of your life, there is a constant and on-going transformation that it produces in the region of your thoughts. As a child of God, you cannot afford to subject your mind to constant speculation and assumptions. Our salvation hinges on our faith in

God who is all knowing and perfect in His ways. We believe him absolutely and do not doubt His word as absolute truth. This way, we can put our trust in His word and believe that we will not be disappointed in any way.

In 2 Corinthians 4:3-4, the scripture talks about the devil trying to blind the minds of people to prevent them from benefiting from God's word. Look at what has happened to the human mind. People are lost because they do not know the gospel, which is the Good News. The Good News is what Jesus Christ brought for the well-being of humanity. God's divinity came down to infuse Himself into humanity.

Many people become born-again, but do not know how to live the spiritual life and still function fully in the natural human realm so they do not prosper to the degree that God intends and achieve their life expectations.

Chapter Three

The Word As a Mirror

"But we all, with an open face beholding as in a glass the glory of the lord, are changed into the same image from glory to glory, even as by the spirit of the lord"

2 Corinthians 3:18

THE SPIRIT EMPOWERING LIFE

Just as a mirror gives a reflection of our physical image, the Word of God provides a reflection of our spiritual image. The more we read and study God's word, His image is replicated in us so we can act just as He would in a given situation. I remember as a young believer in Christ, during which time I was still in high school, I experienced my first miracle. A classmate who was into drugs started hallucinating intensely and hearing voices. Since I had experienced the same challenge as a drug user in the past, I immediately knew the root of his problem. It was the drugs he was using that had opened him up to such demonic attack. I organized some of the Christians on the school campus and we fasted and prayed for our mate.

On the second day of the prayer, the Holy Spirit whispered to me that I should lead him to accept Christ as his Savior and Lord. After he accepted Christ, we commanded the demons to leave him alone and he was set free from those drug demons.

As we fellowship with God through listening, studying the word of God and frequent prayer, the power in God's word transforms us from our fleshly carnal nature into our spirit form. The Apostle Paul says in the scripture above that the word is like a mirror and the more we look at ourselves in the mirror we are transformed into that same image.

This transformation comes through the power of the Spirit of the Lord God Almighty. You cannot ignore the word of God and become what God wants you to become. God used his word to create the world and he uses his word as a change agent to transform us. Without careful study and meditation on the word of God, it will be difficult to know the mind of God and be changed into that image.

The Spirit and the Soul

"In whom the God of this world hath blinded the minds of them which believe not, lest the light of the glorious gospel of Christ, who is the image of God, should shine unto them"
2 Corinthians 4:4

I got saved during the Charismatic Revival wave in the 1980's in my home country Ghana in West Africa. Before this time, people who were Christians were mostly in the well established orthodox churches in the nation. The charismatic revival attracted most of the members of these churches, especially the youth, due to the vibrancy and expression of the Holy Spirit in the charismatic churches. These orthodox churches were plagued by spiritual coldness. Most of them had developed methods and traditions that were totally contrary to faith and having a personal relationship with Christ.

The Charismatic Revival attracted the youth of these orthodox churches who were hungry for a dynamic relationship with God. Initially, most people who transitioned from these churches were very zealous and excited about their discovery and their freedom in the spirit. This was characterized by the baptism of the Holy Spirit with the evidence of speaking in other tongues. With time however, their zeal for spirituality died down and then they began to crave the liturgy of their previous orthodox traditions.

It will amaze you to know that there are people in life-changing-ministries who are participating in everything the ministry is involved in but cannot benefit from the grace over the ministry. They get stuck in the liturgics they were familiar with.

The grace over a ministry can only have an effect on you if you connect to it by revelation and not by tradition. It is crucial to understand this cardinal principle of spiritual renewal which is based on faith in the power of God and not humanistic ideologies and traditions. One can be in a church where revival is taking place and still be lost. The Apostle Paul says the letter kills but the spirit gives life.

"Who also hath made us able ministers of the New Testament; not of the letter, but of the spirit: for the letter killeth, but the spirit giveth life"

THE SPIRIT EMPOWERING LIFE

2 Corinthians 3:6

To experience the benefits of revival taking place in a Church, it is crucial that you connect with the root of the attitudes that triggers renewal in a believer. Those who are thirsty and hungry for righteousness they shall be filled.

"Blessed are they which do hunger and thirst after righteousness: for they shall be filled"
Matthew 5:6

It is a terrible position where people become trapped with human ideology as a substitute for powerful active faith in God. Instead of the power of the gospel that was preached to them, what traps them is religion that is full of human ideologies.

Humanly speaking, all of us crave a deeper relationship with a deity but we just do not know how to go about it. However because our soul yearns for a pure unadulterated spiritual relationship with a supreme being, most people often confuse the soul and the spirit.

Our human soul is that aspect of our being which houses our mind, will and emotions. This gives us expression, experience and sub-consciousness, but it is different from our spirit by which we relate to God.

Our will must embrace our spirit, which is more in tune with God. When Adam sinned against God in the Garden of Eden, it was because his soul was under siege by the deception of the devil.

The devil attacks our human mind because it is limited in knowledge. Deception is how we become vulnerable to the ploys of the devil. When under the attack of deception, our human mind becomes shrouded in uncertainties and assumptions that are also the roots of fear.

Fear is the opposite of faith and has the potential to quickly drown our belief in God's word. Though Adam had heard from God a word that would place him in dominion over the earth, the devil came in with the ploy of deception to neutralize Adam's faith. The devil succeeded with his agenda so our human mind became blinded to spiritual things. The Apostle Paul says it in 2 Corinthians 4:3&4. *"But if our gospel be hid, it is hid to them that are lost: In whom the god of this world hath blinded the minds of them which believe not, lest the light of the glorious gospel of Christ, who is the image of God, should shine unto them"*

When we become born-again, we are just like a little child who does not know anything spiritually and needs a gradual transformation. Our spirit is already developed like God but our human mind has no clue about our spirituality. Our minds are often limited to information which we access through our five senses – sight, hearing, taste, smell and touch. With the amount of information available in our world today as knowledge, there is absolutely no way we can accumulate all the information to make perfect decisions in every area of our lives.

Our spirit however has this capability of knowing as much as is available for our knowing by the Omniscient Spirit of our God. When we receive and believe in the gospel of Christ, we are changed into that same image from glory to glory. This is where spiritual renewal starts, but there is always a conflict.

While your spirit wants you to pray and is yearning for spiritual nourishment, your human mind tells you to go and play and have fun. While your spirit wants to go to church, your flesh complains you have been to church too much so go party somewhere this weekend. Are you getting the difference? That is where our struggle comes from.

The bible says; *"For the flesh lusteth against the Spirit, and the Spirit against the flesh: and these are contrary the one to the other: so that ye cannot do the things that ye would"* Galatians 5:17. For you to be able to relate to God, you need to accomplish a total revolution in your mind and bring your human mind into subjection of your spirit which is more like God's Spirit.

Spiritual renewal therefore starts from inside out not from outside in. For you to develop spiritually, you have to make a decision. As we have already seen, the god of this world is working to blind the minds of people from receiving the glorious gospel of Christ that brings spiritual illumination.

To change our thought pattern to accommodate God's way of thinking cannot simply be wished. If wishes were horses, everyone will simply take a ride. Change must be done consciously. We are transformed by the renewal of our mind. One cannot sit down and simply desire or wait for the transformation to acquire divine attributes to happen by chance.

We have to make a deliberate effort to push forward for the renewal of our minds. The Apostle Paul told the Philippians, *"I press toward the mark for the prize of the high calling of God in Christ Jesus"* Philippians 3:14.

Transformation takes place when we accept God's word in totality and take it in as a whole food. Most of the foods we eat these days are junk. They look like whole food, but they are not. Whole food designated by a nutritionist is food that has all the nutrients in it. Just as whole food breeds a healthy lifestyle and contributes to proper development of the human body, we need wholesome spiritual food so that we can develop spiritually as children of God.

The Bible says that as new-born babies, we have to desire the sincere milk of the word so that we can grow.

"As newborn babes, desire the sincere milk of the word, that ye may grow thereby"
1 Peter 2:2

God has made it available, but if you do not desire it, you cannot get it. The bible says in Romans 12:1-2, *"I beseech you therefore, brethren, by the mercies of God, that ye present your bodies a living sacrifice, holy, acceptable unto God, which is your reasonable service. And be not conformed to this world: but be ye transformed by the renewing of your mind, that ye may prove what is that good, and acceptable, and perfect, will of God."*

Paul said to the Romans, *"And be not conformed to this world" Romans 12:2.* He is not saying "check yourself out of this world", neither does he imply that we commit suicide and die. What he is saying is that we should not pattern our lives according to the standards and the systems of this world. This world has been contaminated by Satan's philosophies. The standards of this world are what causes us to lose our spiritual vitality and spiritual strength.

Here in the US, where many people claim to be Christian, most people work every day of the week including Sundays which is traditionally reserved for worship. They esteem money more than their relationship with God. They mostly work around the clock. For most of these people, the addition of Sundays to their working routine hardly improves their financial status. Though they work seven days a week, if you ask them to give you a thousand dollars, they will end up telling you stories. If money could save us, God would not have sent Jesus Christ to save us. The bible says, *"We were not redeemed by corruptible things like silver and gold but by the precious blood" 1 Peter 1:18.*

When God sent His Son to this world to die for our salvation, the purpose was to place everything we have previously lacked at our disposal. Having bled to death on Calvary's cross for us, do you think Jesus Christ is unable to provide for us? He has given back to us everything the Devil stole from Adam.

If Christ died for us we do not have to doubt what more he can do for us. He can do far more exceedingly, abundantly above what we can ask or think. Most often, He does things for us before we even think about asking for them. We need to renew our minds from thoughts of depravity and survival and trust God to supply our total needs.

Jesus draws our mind to consider the lovely lilies of the fields which do not spin but are clothed beautifully by the heavenly Father.

"Consider the lilies how they grow: they toil not, they spin not; and yet I say unto you, that Solomon in all his glory was not arrayed like one of these"
Luke 12:27

You are better than all God's creation. You were created to have dominion over all God has created. Emancipate yourself by renewing your mind to align with this truth.

Chapter Four

The Tragedy of the Church

In Romans 12:2, we are admonished that, *"... do not be conformed to this world but be transformed by the renewing of your mind..."*

THE SPIRIT EMPOWERING LIFE

There are certain traditions that become ingrained in our minds as we grow up in life which may appeal to common sense yet opposed to the gospel of our Lord Jesus Christ. Such worldly traditions may continue to plague us after we have become saved and potentially hinder our spiritual growth.

In some movies, the storyline portrays a main character who is out to get the villain. The main character would have good intentions but then would be framed up by the villain and he has to fight for vindication.

Such stories ingrain in our mind an inhibition that you ought to fight vehemently to avenge yourself of those who come against you. When you become saved, it takes a long time to overcome such inhibitions. Some believers, even after so many years of being saved still hold on to these vices, which are contrary to biblical truth. As a result, they struggle to align themselves with the spirit of God to help them renew their minds from such old ideas.

Another common example is that some think by working hard they can become financially sound, and they work long hours to overcome poverty. Though there is an element of truth in hard work as one of the keys to success, hard work does not always translate into financial prosperity or else all the hard workers on this earth will be automatically rich. God's Word, in Deuteronomy 8:18 says *"But thou shalt remember the LORD thy God: for it is he that giveth thee power to get wealth, that he may establish his covenant which he sware unto thy fathers, as it is this day."*

Jesus himself said, we make the word of God of no effect because of our traditions. There are many things that we desire and pray for, which God has already answered, but we need to have a renewed mind to receive them.

The human mind is so complex that it takes conscious effort and determination to undo what has been fed to it in a life time. Our mind has been so blinded that when God says He will address our concerns, some cannot even believe it, so we revert to things and behaviours that hinder supernatural solutions. That is the tragedy of the church.

Though the gospel is available to all of us, many do not study it to know the promises of God so when trapped in circumstances, we are unable to act. The reason we cannot experience the goodness of God is because we have not applied our lives to the counsel of God's word.

We often quote the word but because the word of God is not applied to our lives, we still carry around problems that ought not to remain in our lives. He says, *"And be not conformed to this world: but be ye transformed by the renewal of your mind, that you may prove what is that good and acceptable and perfect will of God" Romans 12:2.* Do we not still struggle with that? We have been in church for many years but we still struggle with what God's will is.

As a child of God, you must know what the will of God is for your life. It is part of your development process to quickly learn the way God leads his children or else you will fall prey to the devil. There is God's perfect will which can be found in His word as we delve deep into it and there is the permissive will, which may be allowed by God.

The Perfect Will and Permissive Will of God

"All things are legitimate [permissible—and we are free to do anything we please], but not all things are helpful (expedient, profitable, and wholesome). All things are legitimate, but not all things are constructive [to character] and edifying [to spiritual life]"
1 Corinthians 10:23 (AMP)

As a believer, there are basic things God has already made available to us through the sacrificial death, burial and resurrection of Christ. We are entitled to all the blessings of God, like good health, being successful in every aspect of our lives and many more blessings which come with our submission to Christ. When it comes to the will of God, the believer has the word of God as a guide to make good decisions.

However, there are also more complex decisions, which are not clearly stated in the scriptures. In such instances, we are expected to make decisions based on our knowledge of the word of God and by the conviction of the Holy Spirit. We have to know what God wants and what He accepts.

We also have to know His perfect will, which is different from His permissive will. What is His perfect will and what is his permissive will; one may ask? For example, when someone applies to various colleges and has been admitted to all of the colleges of his choice with scholarship, he still needs to figure out God's choice for him. Even though he has the opportunity, making the choice is now up to him to pursue his career in the college that will best suit him and will bring the best of God's potential out of him.

The choice of career is another dilemma most believers face. Instead of choosing a career that complements their assignment in life, they may end up pursuing a career which pays more money because this is conventional wisdom. Also in this instance, it is not written in the scriptures what the will of God is, so God's will has to be sought prayerfully to obtain conviction.

Another example is a case where a young woman has three suitors who are seeking her hand in marriage. All three of them are good people, hardworking and meet most of her aspirations for a life partner. This is certainly a difficult position to be in and so she would have to definitely seek God's perfect will for her life. She needs to prayerfully ask God's direction in making the right choice, since her marriage will either allow her to be able to fulfil her life purpose or sway her away from that purpose.

God's perfect will is what He has planned from the foundation of the world, and this can be found by seeking God prayerfully. He said, *"I know the thought I think towards you, thoughts of good not of evil, to bring you to an expected end"* Jeremiah 29:11. God has retrofitted you for his purpose so that following his perfect will brings joy and peace of mind. There is nothing gratifying like knowing that you are in the centre of God's will for your life.

Most often, because we are lazy in seeking God's will, in the face of difficult choices we result to the most convenient decisions. Instead of His perfect will, we resort to our own devises and allow His permissive will to prevail. Instead of doing exactly what God would have for our lives, because we choose the most convenient route, he flows with the choices we make. In other words, He permits it. For instance, God may want you to be a pastor and preach his word, but you may want to become a medical doctor instead. In situations like this, God will not strive with you. Even though He may allow you to go ahead if you insist to pursue a career in becoming a medical doctor, that is not His perfect will for you.

As you pursue your relationship with Him, He may eventually spin things around to finally enable you fulfil the mission of becoming a pastor. Ultimately, He will make everything work together for your good, but how awesome will it be when we know specifically what to do when it comes to his will for our lives.

Our God is so merciful that sometimes, in our mistakes, He would work around that to bring us to where He wants us to be. But for us to enjoy the best that God has to offer, we have to follow His perfect will. We have to follow what God accepts of us, we have to know what God approves of us, we have to know what God's perfect will is and just do it.

Some Christians do not know the right from wrong anymore, because we are so plugged into this world's system that when we are wrong, we think we are doing the right thing! Good is now evil and evil has become good. All around us, both inside and outside of the Church we find people indulged in perversions of all kinds. There is spiritual apathy and moral decadence everywhere in society. Check around you! Unfortunately, we do not see anything wrong because compromise and apostasy has become the new norm.

Spiritual maturity comes from knowing what is good and doing it. If you know what is good and you do not do it, what is the use of knowing it anyway? We would have to change the way we view life and the world around us as God's children. The systems of this world are not favorable to our cause, they work hard to distract us from fulfilling our God given purpose. The only way we can effect change in our lives and the world around us is by subscribing to the infallible word of God, submitting our will and action to it to transform us, so that the world around us can also change.

With the realization that we are spirit beings, comes also the need to change into the image of God's Son. We are pilgrims passing through this earth and we need to demonstrate to the world that it is possible for God to work through ordinary people to accomplish extraordinary things.

This earth is not our ultimate home; we are here to make an impact. We must leave a mark by the time we are ready to go. We need to do things that will bring glory to God because without them, we just exist like everyone else. It is so sad to know that there are many people who lived on earth, possessed every resources God provided and died without an impact on society and yet they had great potentials. God wants you to know that he has placed enough glory in you and you have to manifest that glory. *"But we have this treasure in earthen vessels, that the excellency of the power may be of God, and not of us" 2 Corinthians 4:7.*

His investment in us is his glory and we become significant in life when we manifest the glory of God in us. We can manifest that glory by constantly renewing our spirit and allowing the God in us to be revealed. That is possible when we renew our minds so that we may be able to live out the good, acceptable and perfect will of God.

Chapter Five

THE SPIRIT EMPOWERING LIFE

Role of the Word of God

"Study to show thyself approved unto God, a workman that needed not to be ashamed, rightly dividing the word of truth"
2 Timothy 2:15

What can help you to mature quickly as a child of God is the word of God. In some local Churches today, there are some very dynamic prayer warriors who can pray all night till daybreak. They have spiritual intensity and are anointed, but some of them do not know good from evil or right from wrong.

Also, there are some who will not pray at all, but expect to hear from God. They often are unable to discern and know the perfect will of God because they do not know the scriptures. I am not saying this to discourage prayer or long hours of prayer. As a matter of fact, prayer is also one of the key ingredients that helps spiritual renewal.

As it is said in James 5:16-17 (AMP) *"Confess to one another therefore your faults (your slips, your false steps, your offenses, your sins) and pray [also] for one another, that you may be healed and restored [to a spiritual tone of mind and heart]. The earnest (heartfelt, continued) prayer of a righteous man makes tremendous power available [dynamic in its working]. Elijah was a human being with a nature such as we have [with feelings, affections, and a constitution like ours]; and he prayed earnestly for it not to rain, and no rain fell on the earth for three years and six months."* If a man's prayer can stop rain from falling, you can see how powerful an earnest prayer is.

THE SPIRIT EMPOWERING LIFE

In this instance, I am talking about combining prayer with the Word of God. A balanced life is a life we need to transcend the natural. A balanced life also transcends the spiritual, despite that God created you in His image and likeness. You are a spirit but you live in a physical body. Your spirit needs an expression in the physical to be effective because without that you will have an imbalanced life.

You have to be able to balance your spiritual life with your natural life. For instance, if you have to give your young children breakfast, you cannot stay in bed praying whilst they are hungry, all in the name of waiting on the Lord. If you do that, your children will eventually grow to dislike the God who takes up your time and delays their breakfast. If you have to serve breakfast at 6am, you pray long before 6am.

Just as much as prayer has its place in our spiritual growth, the word of God is what throws in the ultimate balance to our spiritual development. You cannot esteem one above the other. With prayer, you have energy to execute the mind of God. But without adequate knowledge of the word of God, you have energy without direction, which is a tragedy. Prayer will give you zeal for God and spiritual intensity, but the word of God will give you knowledge and the direction to apply your zeal appropriately.

THE SPIRIT EMPOWERING LIFE

God wants us to know His word. The word of God helps us to properly define situations in our mind. Your spirit is where God downloads all His intents and purposes and not your mind. Your spirit informs your mind which is in your soul, and your mind informs the brain, which is just in the physical to help you determine how to react or act. So the order in which it works is, spirit, soul and body. If your mind is not properly renewed, you cannot properly define situations based on God's perspective and you will still struggle to live a spiritual life.

An example is when you receive a conviction in your spirit to give an offering. Your spirit did not argue with God about the instruction but then your mind struggles with the spiritual revelation. Your mind is not renewed and so it blocks this message and tells you, "Oh, you have all these bills to pay this week". You then draw the conclusion that you will run out of money. So you do not obey the voice of the spirit - that is carnal thinking. It is carnal because as a child of God you are supposed to be led by your spirit and not by reasoning.

When our minds have not been renewed by God's word, we often act carnally rather than spiritually. God's word produces the renewal of our minds that position us to enjoy the fullness of God's love in every area of our lives. We need to be spiritually renewed because when the Holy Spirit prompts us, it is to bring our life into alignment with God's good plan.

Most often, there is a domino effect of one single act of obedience. When the Holy Spirit says, "do this", it is a set up that triggers something else for us. Our refusal to obey that particular instruction blocks us from experiencing the next level of blessings that lay in the chain of orchestration.

God is looking out for mature men and women to use, not babies. We have too many spiritual babies in the Kingdom of God. In the Church today, there are a lot of spiritual babies moved by emotions and by impulse rather than the word of God or the inner voice of the spirit. That is why some crooked pastors and spiritual leaders can manipulate God's people. They see a lot of ignorance and use it to their advantage. Instead of teaching the truth and telling what God's word says sincerely, they play on the ignorance of people to achieve their personal goals.

I have witnessed occasions where some people claiming to be ministers of the gospel say to a believer: "Sister, I see something in your future ... a black power at work against your life... and the Lord is telling me if you sow a $1000 seed right now, the Holy Ghost will deliver you." Who said that is how the Holy Spirit works? Where is it to be found in the Bible? But then, she will believe that lie than the teaching of truth to overcome any difficulties she might be experiencing in life.

That minister could have honestly said "Sister, we need a projector for the church, is there any way God can touch your heart to bless the church?" Are you getting the difference? She will give $1000 for lies but for the truth, she may only give $20. We need to be renewed to know that when God prompts us, He has a better plan in mind for us.

The Bible says, *"Ye shall know the truth, and the truth shall make you free" John 8:32.* And *"My people are destroyed for lack of knowledge: because thou hast rejected knowledge, I will also reject thee, that thou shalt be no priest to me: seeing thou hast forgotten the law of thy God, I will also forget thy children" Hosea 4:6.* The scripture making us free, is allowing the Spirit of God and our spirit to be in an alignment, allowing ourselves to be led by the Spirit of God instead of human manipulation or our fallen nature.

David prayed to God and said, *"Create in me a clean heart, O God; and renew a right spirit within me" Psalm 51:10.* You do not want to miss God by not following his instructions. Your breakthrough in life is dependent on your obedience to the 'Rhema' word of God.

Yes, the word comes through prophecy, but how do you know the prophecy is inspired by God if you do not know the word of God? You need to have enough knowledge in God's word to differentiate between true and false prophecy. Most Christians have been misled because they did not know when it was the word of God or man trying to manipulate the situation to their advantage.

Chapter Six

THE SPIRIT EMPOWERING LIFE

Understanding Worship

"For God is the King of all the earth: sing ye praises with understanding"

Psalm 47:7

THE SPIRIT EMPOWERING LIFE

In Africa when there is a durbar of chiefs and their people, it is climaxed by the performance of a special dance. You cannot dance anyway and anyhow. Special people are trained to dance while the chief is decorated and seated up on high. People would come and show their loyalty and allegiance by performing special dances. Those dances are done vigorously and intensely. It is sad that when we come before the King of Kings and the Lord of Lords, people want to be pushed to dance in adoration for God.

This is God, the one who created the heavens and the earth. Our faith in Him is why we have to praise Him with understanding. We have to demonstrate appreciation of all that He has done, what He is doing and what He will do and praise Him accordingly. God is worth our fellowship. That is what the word instructs us to do. Never worship because somebody is compelling you. The excuse some of us give is, "I am shy", I hear that a lot. When the mind is supernaturally renewed we worship with the understanding that God is the only one we can fully depend on at all times. We have to believe that if everyone abandons us in life, we shall not be without comfort because God will never leave us nor forsake us. That is what his word promises us. How they behave off the church premises shows whether they are genuinely shy or not. You see them in another setting and you wonder, "Is this the same person who said they are shy?" Shy in the house of God, but outside the house of God, they are not. That is what is known as hypocrisy. You have given us a front that you are shy but when you are out there, you are a different person.

God wants us to live a life of true worship. That is what I want to be for the rest of my life. I do not want to give people what I do not have. If I do not have it, I do not have it, but if I have it, I will give it my all. *"For God is the King of all the earth: sing ye praises with understanding" Psalm 47:7. "Give unto the LORD the glory due unto his name; worship the LORD in the beauty of holiness" Psalm 29:2.* If there is anyone you should give your strength to, it is the one who gave you life. When we learn to give to God what He requires from us, we gain his trust to release to us his treasures.

CHAPTER SEVEN

Importance of the Word of God

In John chapter six, Jesus was speaking about His Godly nature when He realized that His followers were murmuring against Him. They could not understand when He told them He had come down from Heaven, because they could point to His earthly parents. He said to them, *"what then if you should see the Son of man ascend where He was before?"* Jesus continues to explain, *"... The words that I speak to you are spirit, and they are life."* He was talking to them about spiritual things but they could not grasp it.

Many of His followers deserted Him because they could not understand His message to them. To be spiritually renewed or matured requires embracing the word of God as absolute truth. We cannot grow up above our natural acumen if we do not embrace the word of God as absolute truth.

The word of God becomes the renewal agent God uses to change us. He uses the Word in all His exploits so if you do not have the word of God, it will be difficult to experience supernatural change. We cannot achieve anything supernaturally until we apply ourselves to change how we do things to align with God's word. *"Through faith we understand that the worlds were framed by the word of God, so that things which are seen were not made of things which do appear" Hebrews 11:3.*

Change is a reality that we cannot hide from. The world around us is constantly changing and we have no choice but to succumb to these changes. Technology and the systems by which society functions are also ever changing. Some few years ago, cell phones were like radio boxes. You had to carry them on your shoulders to make or receive a call. It was not uncommon in New York, where I live, to find some passengers on the subway turn on their radios which was a nuisance to other passengers. Now we have earphones for a tiny MP3 devise that you can put in your ears so that you alone can hear it.

Life is developing, things are changing and we have to change as God's children. To benefit from God spiritually, we have to make it our goal to change, to grow, to mature, to develop and to be renewed as God's children.

Hebrews 4:12 says, *"For the word of God is quick, and powerful, and sharper than any two edged sword, piercing even to the dividing asunder of soul and spirit, and of the joints and marrow, and is a discerner of the thoughts and intents of the heart"*

The word of God is powerful and sharper than any two-edged sword, separating the aspects of our very being. Bone and marrow is in the physical body. You do not have bone and marrow in your soul. The verse relates to both your spiritual and your physical being. If the word of God can separate the spirit from your soul, which is difficult to distinguish, then it means the word of God can help us to know when our flesh or our spirit is at work.

Without the word of God, nothing can distinguish the soul from the spirit. Medical Doctors, Surgeons or Psychologists are not able to. You are a spirit created in the image and likeness of God. God breathed into moulded dust and it became a living soul. The dust is just what we see on the surface. It is the part we often focus on polishing and developing. Then it gets so puffed up with all that we want everyone to see of us. With time we grow old, die, and go back into the earth. The real you, which is your spirit, will live on forever. So which one do we have to develop more, our spirit or our body?

Therefore the word of God is essential to you as a spirit, who possesses a soul and lives in a physical body. What makes you emotional is your soul. You would be surprised to know that God is emotional too. The Bible says He is a jealous God. If the Bible says, *"grieve not the Holy Spirit"*, it shows that God is emotional. So if He created us in His image and likeness, He wants to tell us that we can live in this physical state and act just like Him.

That is why Jesus came actually to show us how to live. He lived just like you and I, but the Bible says He was without fault because He was not of the attitude of Adam. He came to demonstrate the life of God that is possible even with our humanity.

Do not be overly excited when you see superstars on television with make-up that makes them look picture-perfect. They have problems that overwhelm them like any one of us. That is why many of them get involved with alcohol and drugs, because at the end of the day their strength is limited to the natural. We all have potentially a strength that goes beyond the natural. The Lord promises that he will be with us in times of trouble and out of trouble; he will deliver us. As a child of God you do not develop your life only according to the systems and standards of this world. You develop it according to the word of God.

Chapter Eight

THE SPIRIT EMPOWERING LIFE

Memorize and Meditate on the Word of God

"This Book of the Law shall not depart from your mouth, but you shall meditate in it day and night, that you may observe to do according to all that is written

in it. For then you will make your way prosperous, and then you will have good success"

Joshua 1:8

Goats and cattle have an interesting way of grazing. It is said that they have multiple stomachs into which they chew their food. They bring out the food they have already swallowed, chew it again and put it in their second stomach. They continue with the process until all the food goes to the rightful spaces. This is called, chewing the curd. This is what meditation is like.

To maximize the acquisition of the Word, you need to do certain things on a daily basis. When you wake up every morning, you need to memorize the word, meditate on it, speak it and apply it during the day. Memorization and meditation are two different words. Memorization means you learn by rote. Meditation makes the word a part of your knowledge base. Most people memorize scripture and can quote it verbatim, but they cannot live it because they do not meditate on it.

If you learn John 3:16, *"For God so loved the world that He gave His only begotten son, that whoever believes in Him should not perish but have everlasting life"*, but you do not meditate on it, you will know that scripture verbatim but you may not be saved.

But if you meditate on the words, it will take on a deeper meaning for you. It says, *"God so loved the world"*, and so you begin to understand how God sees you. If you can recite this scripture and still think you are unlovable, then it is apparent that you do not understand the scripture you are quoting. For God so loves you that He gave Christ to save you. If you know *"for God so loved the world,"* do not ever think that nobody loves you.

The devil is a liar and will try to tell you that no one loves you. No one? God loves you! He loves you so much that He sent His son to come and die for you. Those who still entertain doubts about how special they are in the sight of God have memorized that scripture, but have not meditated upon it.

Memorization and meditation on the word are required as a daily exercise because, what you do everyday becomes a habit. Most of us have quite a number of things that have become part of our lives because we have done them over and over and over, and now we cannot stop doing them.

Some of the things that have become part of our lives are good. On the other hand, some of the things that have become our habits may not be helpful, so we want to change them and yet we are not able to do so. This is because they have become a part of us. They say old habits die hard, so if you learn a good habit, it will take you to eternity.

Do not always be quick to jump to things that will set you up to fail. Settle for things that are beneficial, whether you like them or not, whether you feel like it or not. Remember that life here on earth prepares you for eternity. Memorize God's word so when you want to witness to someone, you will be able to know and remember where it is in the Bible. For you to live by it, you have to meditate on it.

Memorize and meditate on the word daily. Have your own routine to spend time with the word of God. Some do it early in the morning, others in the afternoon and some do it just before going to bed. Choose your own comfortable time. Meditate and memorize a scripture which catches your attention. Mark it and underscore it. There are a lot of gadgets these days to help you retain the word of God.

You can have a Bible application on your phone. You can highlight the appropriate verse and once a while, take a peek at it and start saying it to yourself over and over again. This can be done even while working. When you speak the words over yourself, you are renewing your spiritual life.

Psalm 39:3 teaches us that something happens to us as we meditate on God's word. *"My heart was hot within me, while I was musing, the fire burned. Then spake I with my tongue."* That is why the Bible says that out of the abundance of the heart, the mouth speaks. In times of trouble the word comes to your rescue.

You do not speak of the physical appearance of your problems. You speak what you want into situations when you are in difficulty. If I do not have money, I do not say, "I am broke"! You must not say that I am broke. You are not broke! You just do not have the money. The fact that I do not have that money at that particular time does not make me a poor person. You know what makes a person poor? It is the mentality and the mind-set of the person. So you need to renew your mind. If you do not have it, you simply do not have it. You cannot give people what you do not have, so the point is, you do not have it yet.

As the scripture points out, the heart responds to musing the word. The word musing means, to say something to oneself in a thoughtful manner. Musing or meditation establishes things in your spirit when

THE SPIRIT EMPOWERING LIFE

you speak the word over your spirit again and again. Your soul catches it to a point that even in difficulty, you cannot doubt.

How often times many of us have come to a position where we feel unable to accomplish a task, but then something inside us indicates that we cannot go down without a fight. Have you come to that point before? It is not you. It has nothing to do with your brain. It has all to do with your spirit. The investments you have made over the years into your spirit will respond to situations at particular times.

If we are not renewed spiritually, we cannot manifest the glory of God that is inside us. Take all the principles and make sure you apply them. While you are doing that you are reinforcing your spiritual strength for becoming successful.

Someone once made a pertinent comment. He said, becoming successful is not as difficult as maintaining the success. When you allow God to take you through the step-by-step process of becoming successful, He also builds you up to maintain the success. These are principles that can help you become successful and also to retain your success.

Chapter Nine

Speak the Word of God

We must speak the word daily. Meditation helps us to plant the word as seeds in us but after the seeds have been planted in us, we have to speak it. That is the essence of the scripture that says *"out of the abundance of the heart the mouth speaks."* That is why you do not want to be saying things to jinx yourself. You do not want to be saying things to curse your own self. If you speak the word over your life repeatedly, the word of God will renew your spirit and by the time you realize it, you are acting as the word says.

Psalm 45:1 says, *"My heart is overflowing with a good theme."* What does your heart overflow with? Negativity? If your heart is full of a good theme, your expressions will reflect just that. There are people who have been through dangerous ordeals, yet you speak to them and they are so sweet! They do not allow their experiences to define them.

We sometimes allow our experiences to define us. You were successful before. Yes you can be successful again. They hurt you before? Listen! You are still alive and they cannot hurt you again. Move on! Spiritual renewal relates to growth, we need to grow. Every child of God needs to develop.

Create a positive atmosphere. When the atmosphere is right, people will thrive. The scripture says *"my heart is overflowing with a good theme,"* so any time something good comes out of your heart, speak it. When you wake up in the morning and feel good, say it. When you feel something good is going to happen, speak it out. Speak the word over your life to take advantage of the prevailing circumstances. Embrace the positive aspects of life till they become part of you, so that when the negative time comes, you would not be down. *2 Corinthians 4:11 "For we which live are always delivered unto death for Jesus' sake, that the life also of Jesus might be made manifest in our mortal flesh."*

When we come together, our spirits bear witness with each other. We should love each other unconditionally. Our attitude to one another in times of difficulty should be, "brother, what situation are you going through for which we should agree with you in prayer?" It should not be, "oh he has been around for so long but nothing good is happening to him". We are to speak encouraging words to each other, speak God's word into every situation and not accept the condition of unfavourable circumstances.

The environment of believers should be a place where people hold each other's hands, laugh and rejoice with one another. When our heart is overflowing with good things, it overshadows situations that may not be pleasant. This way, negative situations no longer generate negative impacts on us. Not quite long ago, Americans in the northeast were panicking about super-storm 'Sandy' as it approached land from the sea. As predicted, it did quite a lot of damage to lives and properties in its way. But after the damage it was time to gain the strength to work. It was time to repair what could be repaired and restore what could be restored and to allow God to do the rest.

Will you give up because of one experience? We, in America, are spoilt, right? In Africa, there are people who carry their wares on their heads with babies tied to their back and yet selling across streets! Over here in the US, people have credit cards and access to government welfare programs, but still complain about the basic things in life. We need renewal in our minds to appreciate even the little things that God does for us.

"We having the same spirit of faith, according as it is written, I believed, and therefore have I spoken; we also believe, and therefore speak"
2 Corinthians 4:13

The scripture here says we have the same spirit of faith. The spirit you have is the same spirit I have. It further encourages us to speak, based on our faith. It is therefore not appropriate for Christians to speak negative words based on prevailing situations. Believers are enjoined to express their faith. That faith is based on the spirit we received from God when we believed.

THE SPIRIT EMPOWERING LIFE

A saying goes:
Watch your thoughts, they become your words
Watch your words, they become your actions
Watch your actions, they become your habits
Watch your habits, they become your character
Watch your character and it contributes to your life's outcome!

How true that the Bible has already identified the moral that this saying is trying to teach! The words we speak are born from within us. But very importantly, our words have a bearing on the outcome of our lives!

It is written in Psalm 116:10, *"I believed therefore I spoke."* So when you speak to another believer, your faith should be revealed. We believe and so we speak. Some have the habit of saying the negative and when you question them, they say, "Oh I was just joking."

Our speech is very powerful! You are reducing or increasing your own creative ability by what you say. If you want God to work on your behalf, first work on what you say. Whatever you say empowers God to work or not to work on your behalf. Say what you mean!

Chapter Ten

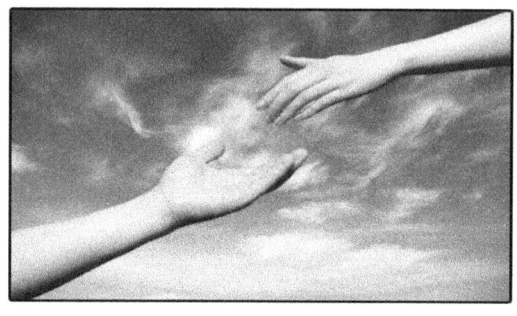

Apply the Word of God

"This book of the law shall not depart out of thy mouth; but thou shalt meditate therein day and night, that thow mayest observe to do according to all that is written therin: for then thou shalt make thy way prosperous, and then thou shall have good success"
                                                Joshua 1:8

The next point is to apply the word daily. First, memorize the word of God. Second, meditate on it daily. Third, you need to speak the word daily. Finally, to complete the process, you need to apply the word daily. Do you know that the things you do not practice do not become part of you?

You have been taught how to drive a car, but you do not practice it. When you get a car and you have difficulty driving it, you would think the one who taught you did not teach you well. The problem is that you did not practice what you were taught, though he may have taught you the right way. So it is important to apply the word.

Do not let these words be in vain. Apply them and memorize the words. You may not need them right now because today everything is dandy for you. But tomorrow, something could happen and you would realize that the word of God that you have studied would come to the rescue. This is when God's word becomes a source of direction and inspiration in difficult times.

Speak and apply the word daily. It is not difficult as most of us think. When you go to bed at night, you try to think about the word that you memorized during the day. When we were younger, there was not much technology so we wrote the word on postcards and kept them in our pockets. We read them from time to time and put them back in our pockets.

You may not see the effects immediately, but after sometime, those words come back. Your memory should have a healthy bank account, to store all the good things that you are learning. If you do not feed your mind with good things, you will not manifest good things. Someone once said, "you have to change your mind like you change your clothes" as in renewing the mind. Do not sit around harbouring negative thoughts. Negative thoughts breed negative behaviour. If you think so much about evil things you will realize that your life will take that turn into negativity.

"Whatever things are true, whatever things are noble, whatever things are just, whatever things are pure, whatever things are lovely, whatever things are of good report, if there is anything praiseworthy, meditate on these things"
Philippians 4:8

Do not be thinking of people who do not like you. If they do not like you, you cannot do anything to change it. Move on. Do not hate them either, because it is not healthy. So if that thought comes into your mind, quickly change it. Do not think about that, focus on good things.

Harness on 'wow'! This person likes me, what can I do to let them know I like them back?' Think of good things. Think of things that are honest. James 1:22 says, *"But be ye doers of the word and not hearers only, deceiving your ownselves"* It further elaborates, *"If anyone is a hearer of the word and not a doer, he is like a man observing his natural face in a mirror; for he observes himself, and goes away, and immediately forgets what kind of man he was."*

We all use the mirror. The mirror helps us see our faces and other parts of our body that we would not have been able to observe otherwise, thereby helping us dress up the way we want to. But for those who fail to do the word of God, the scripture says he immediately forgets what kind of man he was after observing himself.

Therefore, the scripture elaborates on the right attitude with the word of God, *"But he who looks into the perfect law of liberty and continues in it, and is not a forgetful hearer, but a doer of the work, this one will be blessed in what he does."*

The most difficult part is how to apply the word. You know this group of people do not like you, but you have to minister to them anyway. Ministering to people is a duty call from God and does not depend on who likes you and who hates you.

Applying the word is the most difficult part of our Christian walk, and that is what changes you, not the people. Jesus was amongst human beings. He was among people just like us in these days. But the Bible says He never hated anybody. The very people He intended to die for were the very people who crucified Him! Yet on the cross, He forgave them all.

The need for spiritual renewal is crucial for every Christian. This renewal takes place in our minds, which tends to be the battleground between good and evil. To win this battle, our chief weapon is the word of God, which we must make a part of us through daily exercise. We need to memorize the word, meditate on the word, speak the word and apply the word.

Applying God's word is how you will unlock your spiritual potential and activate your spiritual energy. You will grow, mature and lead a victorious Christian life. As an effective child of God, you have a heritage of victory through the work of Christ on the cross.

In Isaiah 54:17 scripture identifies your heritage, *"No weapon formed against you shall prosper, and every tongue which rises against you in judgment you shall condemn."* How you handle negative situations will help you to know how to handle success when God brings it your way. You should understand that God wants mature people to work with, not babes in Christ. He wants us to identify with him and all that he did for us. That is the only way we can live the spirit life.

Understand that you are a spirit being and have the image of God residing in you. You possess a soul that gives you the expression and life in a physical body. When we live with only our emotions and the dictates of the physical body, we limit ourselves to the earth realm. When we are able to mortify the body and give our spirit expression, the results can be phenomenal. God is in us, wanting to show off His awesome potentials through our lives.

We are limited when we shut the spirit up and operate just as humans without the influence of our regenerated human spirit. As a matter of fact, the Holy Spirit leads us through our spirit and not our soul. We are sitting in heavenly places with Christ and so we must live our lives from heaven's perspective, not earth's. Christ made us complete in him, so as God's children we will have to learn to acknowledge everything that is in us through Christ. *"In him we live, we move and have our being."*

When we identify with Him, as He was in the world so shall we be in this world.

"We know [understand, recognize, are conscious of, by observation and by experience] and believe [adhere to and put faith in and rely on] the love God cherishes for us. God is love, and he who dwells and continues in love dwells and continues in God, and God dwells and continues in him. In this [union and communion with him] love is brought to completion and attains perfection with us, that we may have confidence for the day of judgement [with assurance and boldness to face him], because as he is, so are we in this world"

1 John 4:16-17 (AMP)

We need to renew our minds to think and act as Jesus was, when he was in the world. All that he did affected us, spirit, soul and body. We must acknowledge everything that is in us through Christ. His work on Calvary's cross brought us grace that no hard work can qualify us for. But we need to have faith in what he did to be able to benefit from it. His grace is his greater grip on us and our faith is what makes the connection. Hebrews 11:6 says, *"But without faith it is impossible to please him: for he that comes to God must believe that he is and that he is a rewarder of them that diligently seek him."*

THE SPIRIT EMPOWERING LIFE

When you seek him by faith, your efforts shall be rewarded.

ABOUT THE AUTHOR

Sammy N. Addy is a renowned international speaker whom God has raised in this season to father many in the body of Christ. As an apostle and bible teacher, he also operates in the prophetic anointing.

Apostle Addy is the founder and General Overseer of Wisdom International Network Ministries, an apostolic network of cutting edge ministries and churches based in New York City. He is the Senior Pastor of Wisdom Chapel International. He is also the president of Wisdom Leadership Institute and Wisdom School of Ministry, schools he uses to prepare the next generation of leaders and ministers.

His passion is to educate, motivate and empower leaders, ministers, ministries and believers alike to be all they can be and be able to fulfill their God given assignment.

THE SPIRIT EMPOWERING LIFE

FOR INFORMATION CALL:
Wisdom Chapel International
2941 Boston Road
Bronx, NY 10469
718.515.6211

EMAIL:
wisdomconnection@gmail.com

OR VISIT WEBSITE:
www.wisdomchapelint.org

www.ingramcontent.com/pod-product-compliance
Lightning Source LLC
Chambersburg PA
CBHW060848050426
42453CB00008B/882